Walking and Climbing

Walking and Climbing

Walt Unsworth

London, Henley and Boston
Routledge & Kegan Paul

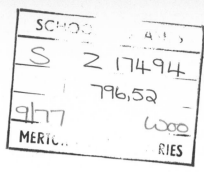
First published in 1977
by Routledge & Kegan Paul Ltd
39 Store Street,
London WC1E 7DD,
Broadway House,
Newtown Road,
Henley-on-Thames,
Oxon RG9 1EN and
9 Park Street,
Boston, Mass. 02108, USA
Filmset and printed in Great Britain by
BAS Printers Limited, Over Wallop, Hampshire
© Walt Unsworth 1977

British Library Cataloguing in Publication Data

Unsworth, Walter

Walking and climbing. — (Local search series).
1. Walking — Great Britain   2. Rock climbing —
Great Britain
I. Title   II. Series
796.5'22   GV199.44.G7

ISBN 0 7100 8596 6

Frontispiece: Using an ice axe as a brake.

Contents

'. . . all the business of life is to endeavour to find out what you don't know by what you do'

John Whiting *Marching Song*

Editor's preface

If you have never lived or spent a holiday near mountains you may not realise the fascination they have for some people; yet to others they are terrifying. Because of their remoteness they have at times, and in different parts of the world, been considered to be holy places, visited by very few people.

This book deals with more accessible mountains – those in Britain which, for their beauty, their interest and their dangers, are appealing to more and more people nowadays. It tells you how to find your way on hills and moorlands, what to look for, what equipment to take and what safety precautions are necessary. And there is a step by step description of actual rock climbing.

Nowadays there is a lot of discussion about the preservation of mountain areas and who should have access to them. In some rocks there are valuable minerals and mining companies want permission from the Government to extract these. Other people object to this and feel strongly that natural, wild places are particularly important nowadays and should be preserved only for people's enjoyment. But already, in some places, so many people are walking and climbing in our wildest, highest areas that paths are being worn down, rocks loosened and vegetation damaged.

So, as well as being there for our enjoyment, mountains present many problems. There is certainly no *one* answer, but we should all think about what we do and act in a responsible way when we go into the countryside and on to the hills.

M.H.

Hills of adventure

What are mountains?

Mountains on maps

Man in the mountains

If you look in an atlas at a map of Britain you will notice that a lot of the land has been coloured brown by the map-maker. Perhaps you know that this brown colouring means high land — hills, moors and mountains? There seems an awful lot of it, especially in the north and west.

You might wonder why it is necessary for the map-maker to show mountains and hills. What difference does it make? Well, if you look closer at the map you will see that there are very few towns and no big cities in the mountains, which means that people have found it hard to live there. The soil is often poor, unsuitable for agriculture; the climate is colder and wetter than it is on the plains; and the steep land makes it difficult for men to build roads and railways. Mountains have always been looked upon as unfriendly to Man and in the old days people who lived in the mountains were regarded as uncivilised — did you know that the word *mountaineer* once meant a savage?

Of course, the word means something quite different today — it means a man who climbs mountains for sport and pleasure. It is only in the last hundred years or so that people began finding pleasure in the hills — walking, climbing, skiing, caving and even newer sports like hang-gliding. The mountains which our forefathers hated have turned into one of our best playgrounds!

Hills, moors and mountains
The map in your atlas tells you where the hills are, but it does not tell you what they are like. Some are really quite small and gentle

and you could run up them in half an hour. They may even be wooded, right to the top, but more than likely they have short, springy turf which is nice to play on. In the south of England the North and South Downs are like this, and the Chilterns and Cotswolds — but there are many more elsewhere. Walking along their crests is easy and pleasant.

Elsewhere the land may rise in larger masses and to greater height; great brooding monsters, all browns and greys, or perhaps patched with purple heather in the late summer. These are the moors, all lumpy and lonely, where sometimes it is possible to wander for hours without seeing another soul. There are no trees except in sheltered nooks, few houses, and the land is rough heather, tussock grass or bog. On the larger moors, such as Dartmoor or Kinder Scout, the wilderness rolls away to the skyline. Sometimes there is a rock pinnacle, called a tor, to break the monotony of the scene.

Gentle hills like the Mendips offer easy walking.

Walking across a moor can often be very tough going. Because there are few landmarks a map and compass are necessary for

navigation. Many people get lost on the moors, and it can be very *Tryfan, in Snowdonia.*
frightening and sometimes dangerous.

In Britain if a hill or a moor rises above 2,000 ft (610 m) in height it
is called a mountain. It may be just a big smooth hill, easy to climb
though possibly taking a long time, like Skiddaw in the Lake
District, or it may be guarded by steep, jagged rocks which make
any way up very difficult, like Tryfan in Snowdonia. Most of our
British mountains are in between these types, that is, they can be
climbed by a track up grassy slopes but have rocks and cliffs
jutting out in places.

British mountains
The highest British mountains are in Scotland — which is why we
talk of 'the Highlands'. Highest of all is Ben Nevis (4,406 ft or

Ben Nevis, the highest mountain in Britain.

Stanage Edge, a famous gritstone crag in the High Peak.

View over Llyn Ogwen.

1,343 m). It can be climbed by a broad track from Glen Nevis and every year there is a race to the summit and back from the nearby town of Fort William. But 'The Ben', as it is called by climbers, has a tougher side to it: on its northern face great cliffs plunge down into the Allt a' Mhuilinn, a lonely glen. In winter, conditions on Ben Nevis can be very severe: there is usually snow on the mountain from November to April or May.

In Scotland there are 279 mountains over 3,000 ft (941 m) high and these are known as Munros, after Sir Hugh Munro who, in 1891, was the first to make a list of them. Many mountaineers have made it a hobby to climb all the Munros.

In the rest of Britain, 3,000-ft peaks are rarer. There are 14 in Snowdonia and 4 in the Lake District. These two areas also have most of the other mountains, too, with the Pennines coming into third place. The highest peak in England is Scafell Pike (3,210 ft or 978 m), in Wales, Snowdon (3,561 ft or 1,085 m) and in Ireland, Carrauntual (3,414 ft or 1,038 m).

What can the map tell us?

If we want to find out what sort of mountains we are dealing with, we need a much larger map than the one in the atlas. In Britain the best large scale maps are provided by a Government Department called the Ordnance Survey. For years, walkers and climbers have relied upon the One Inch, that is, a map where one inch on the map equals one mile on the ground. These are now being replaced by new maps on a scale of 1:50,000 where 1 cm on the map equals 50,000 cm on the ground, or put another way, 2 cm represents 1 km.

The scale is important because it tells us how far we have to walk to get from one place to another. The height we have to climb during the walk is shown by faint lines called contours, which run round the hills on the map. Everywhere on the same contour line is the same height and the lines themselves are 50 ft (15·2 m) apart. So if you walk to the top of a hill and cross ten contour lines on the map in doing so, you have climbed 500 ft (152 m) from the point where you started. Eventually contour lines will be redrawn to take care of metric measure, but this will probably not be for some time

because of the enormous amount of re-drawing the map-makers
will have to do!

Contour lines also show us how steep the ground is. Here is a
simple rule — the wider apart the contour lines, the less steep the
ground and the closer together they are, the steeper the ground.
The diagrams will make this very clear to you.

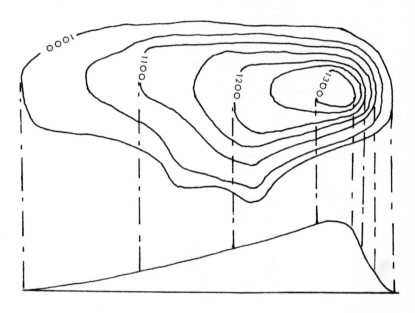

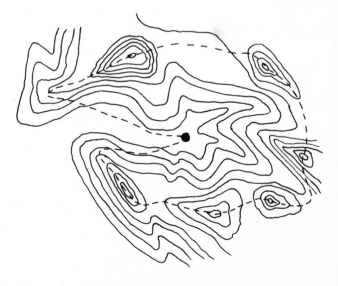

Very often contour lines are shown running from one hill to the next, because hills very often occur in groups. A study of the lines will show that it is possible to walk from one hill to the next without having to descend all the way to the valley — in fact, the drop between one hill and the next might be quite small. Several hills can be climbed in this way for little extra effort, and walking from hill to hill like this is called ridge walking. It is the most popular way of tackling a group of hills.

Symbols on the map

It is not possible to draw everything to the right scale on a map — most buildings, for example, would be so small you could hardly see them. To overcome this, symbols are used. These are easy to understand once you get the idea, and they are shown on the edge of the map just in case you forget which symbol is which. In the mountains, the symbol which shows 'crags' might mean a steep cliff or it might just mean a few broken rocks — but in either case it means watch out, there's danger. The latest maps show rights of way, that is, routes where you can walk without asking anybody's permission. The other tracks shown are not rights of way, though in many cases nobody will object to you using them. If in doubt you should ask locally.

What the hills are made of

People who have used maps a good deal and been walking in the hills can often tell just by looking at the map what the hills are made of. That is, what sort of rock is there. Different types of rock give different scenery. For example, the South Downs are made of chalk, a rock which is easily worn away by the weather, and so, as you might expect, the hills there are round and smooth. On the other hand gabbro is a hard rock and the Cuillin Hills of Skye, which are mostly gabbro, are sharp and spiky. Rock climbers in particular like to know what sort of rock they will encounter on a mountain, and though some climbers will tackle anything, most climbers would object to climbing on a loose rock like shale, or one which easily crumbles, like chalk.

It can be very interesting to collect examples of rocks found on hill

walks and compare one with another. The specimens need not be
big — each can be kept in a matchbox and labelled. There are
several handbooks in the library which will help you to identify the
rocks and you will also be able to collect and identify those rather
special bits of rock called minerals, which occur in mountain areas.
In limestone areas you will also find many small fossils.

Seen in the hills

Because mountains are steep and wild places there are many
wonderful sights to be seen. All our largest lakes are in mountain
areas, and of course Cumbria is actually called the Lake District.
Then too, there are the smaller lakes, or tarns, nestling in between
ridges high up in the mountains and often very beautiful. There is
one tarn in the Lake District which is so deeply set between tall
mountains that for many years the local people believed the sun

*Limestone scenery in
Wolfscote Dale,
Derbyshire.*

The spiky gabbro rock of Sgurr Alasdair in the Cuillins of Skye.

A famous mountain scene in the High Peak. Kinder Downfall with the water being blown back by a high wind.

never shone on it and that you could see the stars reflected in it, even in daytime!

Waterfalls, too, are very common and after heavy rain they look spectacular, and sometimes have a roar that can be heard from quite a distance. In limestone areas you will find caves and pot-holes where underground streams have worn a way through the rock, often for miles. Some of the caves are known as 'show caves' because visitors can be taken round them for a small entrance fee, but many are just open holes in the ground. Never explore caves unless you are with an experienced caver — they can be very dangerous.

Man in the mountains

Though our ancestors were no lovers of mountains, they frequently had to use them either for defence in times of war, or to obtain materials they could not get elsewhere. Traces of these activities can still be seen.

Even as long ago as the Stone Age men were exploring the fastnesses of the Lake District for a pale green tough rock very suitable for making stone axes, and their 'axe factory' as it has been called has been found in Langdale, high up on Pike of Stickle. The surprising thing is that axes from this factory have been found in many parts of Britain, showing that the Langdale axe factory had a thriving export business. Of course, there are other signs of pre-history too: a great many stone circles, and burial mounds or barrows. Some of them are in very bleak places indeed, though long ago they may have been covered in forest.

Roman roads and Roman forts can also be found in our hills, and also the great hill forts of the Dark Ages, like the one on top of Mam Tor in the Peak District. Even those vast defensive works, the Roman Wall and Offa's Dyke, are built mostly in hill and moorland country. The steep nature of hills has always been a defence against attack.

In later years Man came to the hills for stone and for minerals. The quarries can still be seen, many of them now abandoned. Some of them are enormous, like the slate quarries of Llanberis in North Wales (once called the biggest holes in the world!) and they have

Man in the hills. Rough Tor on Bodmin Moor, Cornwall, with the spoils of a china clay works beyond.

left permanent scars on the landscape. Limestone quarries are still being worked because limestone is a valuable rock used for making cement, and in other industrial processes. Some areas, such as part of the Peak District, suffer from the scars of the limestone quarries and the terrible white dust made by the cement factories. Do you think limestone quarries should be allowed in areas of natural beauty? On the one hand they spoil the scenery, on the other they provide jobs in areas where other jobs are hard to come by.

Older industries have died out and their remains are now studied by industrial archaeologists. There are small, ancient mills scattered over the Pennine moors and dating from the time when water power drove the machinery. Some still have mill wheels and it is interesting to work out whether it was an undershot or overshot wheel. Lead mines and copper mines can also be seen in many mountain areas, and it is fascinating to trace out among the tumbled ruins how the ore was crushed and washed and perhaps smelted. Harder to find are the old bloomeries, where iron was made in the days before blast furnaces were invented.

One thing to remember — old quarries and mines are very dangerous. Never, never enter an old mineshaft, and if you are in an area where old lead mines were common watch your step. Some of the shafts are unguarded.

The great variety

Hills, moors and mountains are all things to all men. You can use them for simple walks, enjoying the scenery, or tougher walks which are a challenge. You can tackle the steep crags in the sport of rock climbing or you can hunt for minerals. You can trace out a Roman road or investigate old industries.

Mountains are great fun — but they can be dangerous, and if you want to enjoy them safely, you must learn to tackle them in the right way.

2   Up hill, down dale

Walking in hill country

Bad weather

Map and compass

Gear for walking

Simple valley walks where the paths are good require no special gear. A pair of stout shoes, a light sweater in case the breeze turns cold, and a cycle cape or anorak to ward off the showers are the essentials. Once you start leaving the level paths, however, something better is called for.

The only proper footwear in the hills are boots. Providing they are correctly chosen in the first place, boots are more comfortable than shoes for a long walk, they give protection to the ankles, and they keep the feet dry. They should be bought from a specialist dealer (a mountaineering shop) and not a general shoe shop because then the assistant will be able to advise you on your choice. There are two main types: walking boots, which have a bendy sole, and mountaineering boots, which have a stiffened sole. The walking boots are lighter and cheaper than the others and quite adequate for most people. They will be fitted with a cleated rubber sole called Vibram.

When trying them on you should wear the same sort of socks you intend to walk in and the fit must be comfortable. A good test is whether the boot is firm round the ankle yet with just enough room to wriggle your toes. The shop will advise you how to look after them, but if they get wet (and they will!) never dry them in front of a fire. Perhaps you can think why, and work out some other way of drying them?

Some walkers like to wear two pairs of thick wool socks at a time. The inner pair are long stockings (because they often wear knee breeches) and the outer pair are short socks. Knee breeches give

Typical hill-walking boots.

lots of freedom to your legs, but are not essential. The point to watch here is that the breeches you wear are warm, and for this reason cotton jeans are not satisfactory. They might be all right for a summer's day in the valley or some low hills, but in the bigger hills the drop in temperature when the wind springs up can be surprising.

Exposure

'Wool for warmth' is an old saying with a lot of truth in it. In the hills wool shirts, wool sweaters and wool trousers keep out the cold because wool retains its insulation even when wet. The problem is to keep in body heat, which can soon be lost by a chilling wind, especially in wet conditions. As the body gets colder it doesn't work properly and someone who loses a lot of body heat begins to suffer from exposure. The signs of this are uncontrollable shivering, great tiredness, bad temper, unusual behaviour, slurred speech and, in bad cases, double vision. It is very serious and the treatment is to wrap the victim up as warmly as possible, give him hot drinks and food and, if necessary, send someone for the mountain rescue.

It is the chilling wind which is the chief culprit and so on top of the wool clothes you need something to keep out the wind. If it also keeps out the rain, so much the better, though the perfect waterproof has yet to be invented. The two most common ones are the anorak and the cagoule.

An alpine jacket.

The anorak was invented by the Eskimos and adapted by explorers. The best ones are made of ventile cloth, have a big pouch pocket for maps and have storm cuffs which prevent the wind and rain being blown up your sleeves. However, pulling it on and off over your head can be a nuisance if the weather keeps changing and more recently many outdoor people have gone over

A waterproof cagoule.

to using an alpine jacket, which is really an anorak with a big zipper down the front.

The cagoule is similar to an anorak but longer — it comes down to your knees — and it is made of waterproof polyurethane. It is very light and can be rolled up into a tiny bundle when not in use. The snag is that just as water can't get in, neither can it get out, and perspiration condenses on the inside, so that you are soon damp anyway!

On cold days or when the wind is blowing you will probably find that a balaclava helmet of wool is comfortable and a pair of wool gloves — actually a spare pair of socks will do for the latter in an emergency. The main aim is always to keep warm — keeping dry is not so important.

Common sense
The chief requirement for any adventure in the hills is common sense. Take this business about warm clothing. Obviously on a blazing day in June you would not go hill walking dressed in a thick sweater, anorak and all the rest — you would probably collapse from heat exhaustion! You would set out lightly clad, but you would have the sense to carry extra gear in a rucksack, just in case things turned nasty. Shorts are grand for a hot day, provided you have breeches in the sack as a precaution. Let me ask you a question: did you ever see a shepherd wearing shorts?

Rucksacks
When walking and climbing in rough country it is essential to keep your hands free for the occasional steadying hold. Anything to be carried, must be carried on your back and the bag for this is called a rucksack. There are all sorts or rucksacks, from tiny lightweight day-sacks, which, as their name implies, hold enough for a day's stroll — some sandwiches, a flask and a sweater — up to enormous bags supported on alloy frames, and holding enough for a week's camping, including the tent. Recently, these big bags have become known as backpacks, or pack frames, and anyone who wanders in the hills, self-sufficient to all his needs, is called a backpacker. No one rucksack is suited to every purpose, but most

Backpacking.

An alpine rucksack.

hill-goers plump for a medium-sized bag known as an alpine sack. You can guess why it is called this, I'm sure.

Feed the inner man

A day on the hills requires a lot of energy and so you need to keep your tummy stoked up. Easily digested foods are best — fruit, nuts and raisins, chocolate — but nearly everyone takes sandwiches as well, partly out of habit, I suppose. Make them light ones — chicken, jam, honey. Nothing is more unappetising than thick cheese 'butties' on the hills. It is better to eat small snacks during rest periods than have one big meal at mid-day. Why is this, do you think?

Many walkers seem able to go all day without a drink of any sort but in winter a flask of tea or coffee is very acceptable or in summer a flask of iced fruit drink. Pop is not a good idea: shake up a half empty bottle of pop some day and just imagine what happens inside you as you jog up and down the hills! Drinking from a mountain stream is a risky business because of possible pollution — there could be a dead sheep in it, higher up the hill. Drinking from a valley stream is downright dangerous — you could probably make a list of the sources of infection if you thought about it.

Valley walking

It is possible to be in the hills without actually being on them. Some of the valleys make splendid walks. The first essential is to get off the road and on to paths, and this means using your map. You are not likely to need a compass for a valley walk, because you are confined by the hills, but you may need one if you cross from one valley to another.

Valley walking is easy because there is very little climbing to do — possibly none at all. The Lake District has some beautiful valleys well suited to this sort of walking — Borrowdale, for example, or Dunnerdale. Some can be quite exciting, like crossing the Wastwater Screes, where the path threads cautiously through great blocks of rock. Limestone country often gives exciting valley walks, too: Dovedale in the Peak District is one of the most beautiful valleys in Britain, with fascinating rock pinnacles and

*Hodder Valley in
Bowland: typical hills
for the beginner.*

caves, or there is Gordale Scar in Yorkshire, where the valley is so narrow the immense rock walls seem almost to touch.

Easy hills

Your first excursion into the hills should be to some local heights which are not too difficult to tackle. The aim is not only to enjoy the day out but also to find out how to walk on steep ground without becoming tired. The method is really quite simple: just take it very steadily. A steady pace means you do not need to stop for a rest so often — once an hour should be enough for a beginner, with the rest taking ten or fifteen minutes. Rushing up the hills and stopping for rests every fifteen minutes is the most tiring way of going about the job. Experienced walkers, on the larger hills, often take only a couple of half-hour rests in the course of a day.

These easy days out will also teach you how to discover the right 'line' — that is, the best way to tackle a slope you are climbing. If it is very steep, going straight up might not be a good idea; it might be better to tackle it in a series of wide zig-zags. Can you see how this makes it easier?

If the hill is an easy one, with soft springy turf, it is very tempting to run down, once you have climbed it. This can be very dangerous, especially if there are any crags or quarries round about. It is very easy to run out of control, that is, once you start running you can't stop but just go faster and faster until you take a nasty tumble and end up with a broken arm or worse.

There are lots of easy hills in Britain and unless you live in some particularly flat area, like the Fens, there are bound to be some quite near you. Some can be linked together into marvellous little ridge walks — the Malvern Hills, for example.

One of the problems of walking on these low hills is that of access. Because the hills are not very big, farms and houses creep up their sides making a barrier of hedges and fields. You must find a path through these; you can't just go barging across somebody's field or back garden! Often the path will be signposted and will be a right of way, i.e. a path which anyone has the right to use. The new Ordnance Survey maps show all rights of way.

Using a map and compass
Before venturing on to bigger hills or wild moorland it is useful to know how to use a map and compass. Used together these two will tell you in which direction you should walk, how far it is and what obstacles are in the way.

A map is really a bird's-eye picture of a piece of land, as we have indicated in the previous chapter. The easiest way to use a map when out walking is to line it up with some easily identified objects such as a church steeple and a beacon, then by referring to the map you can learn all you want to know about the land. It may show you, for example, that there is a stream between you and your objective and that the nearest bridge is two miles down river. Obviously, you would alter course to take this into account.

But what about when you are on a wild moorland where there may be no easily identified objects, or when the mist is down and you can't see a thing? This is where the compass comes into its own.

The compass is a magnetic needle delicately pivoted in the middle and protected by a stout transparent case. Because it is a magnet the needle will always point to the north and south magnetic poles of the earth – the north-pointing end is usually coloured. So right away you have a rough idea of position because the map's north is always at the top.

However, the compass can be used much more accurately than that! For good compass work which does not require a lot of fuss and calculating, a Silva type compass is essential. This has a rectangular clear plastic base, called the protractor, upon which the compass is fixed. The figures round the needle, showing degrees, will swivel (see picture).

To use the compass lay the edge of the protractor along the map in the direction you want to travel, and swivel the ring on the compass until the parallel lines marked on it come into line with the grid lines on the map. (These are lines which run N-S and E-W on the map: you want the N-S ones). Now read off the bearing shown by the direction pointer of the protractor. Let us say it is 50°. Now swivel the ring again adding 8° to this, making a bearing of 58°. Now hold the compass so that the needle points to the north mark on the ring, and the direction arrow will show you the direction in which to walk.

This sounds complicated when you read it but it isn't really. Try it out with a map and compass and see how simple it is. You can practise at home or in the classroom – just pretend you are going from one place on the map to another, until the use of the compass becomes automatic.

The next stage is to take your map and compass into some real hills – the low ones which you already know, and put the method to a proper test. See how near you can get to your objective – that will tell you how accurate you were in your compass settings.

One thing which may be puzzling you about using the compass is why do we add 8° to our figures? Perhaps you can guess? Well, the answer is that the grid lines on the map point to Grid North

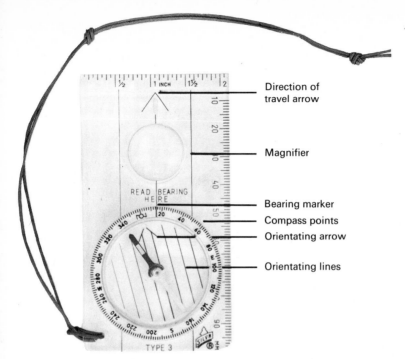

A compass.

Direction of travel arrow

Magnifier

Bearing marker

Compass points

Orientating arrow

Orientating lines

READ BEARING HERE

TYPE 3

(which is near enough to True North) whereas the compass needle points to Magnetic North, and there is a difference of 8° between the two. So after we have set the compass according to the grid lines, we must make allowances for the magnetic variation, as it is called.

Actually the Magnetic North is a funny thing, because it shifts its position a little bit each year – about $\frac{1}{2}$° every five years, in fact, so the variation is 8° in 1977 but will be only 7° in 1987 and so on. Perhaps you have learned about the magnetic poles in your science lessons? Find out what happens once the variation reaches zero!

Well, you might say, this is all very fine, but the fact is that few mountain walks are done in a straight line – there might well be a crag in the way, for instance, or a lake. In that case you break up the route into a series of straight lines (see diagram), resetting the compass for each change of direction. Try to aim for some recognisable feature each time, it makes navigation much simpler and it is very satisfying to arrive bang on target at the end of each leg of the course.

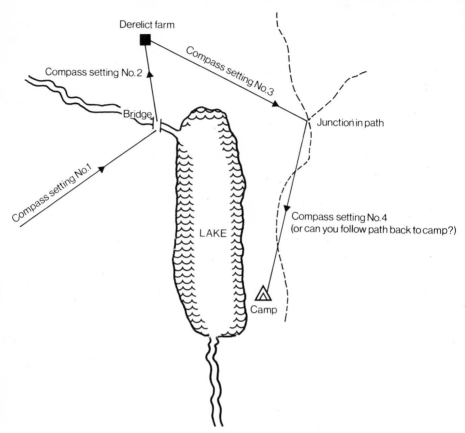

If you can't do this — if you are in the middle of a featureless moor in thick mist, for example — then you certainly have a problem. You must then not only navigate for direction, but for distance too, and the only way of doing this is to count your steps and know in advance just what one average step measures! Perhaps in your maths lessons your teacher will let you pace out ten steps and measure the distance covered — you can then get a good idea of what your average step is.

The compass really is a marvellous little instrument with all sorts of uses — you can find out your actual position on the map, for example, providing you can sight a couple of recognisable landmarks, but I'll let you figure that out for yourselves! There are games which can be played using the compass, too, and a whole sport called orienteering has been built up around map and compass work. It is a sort of cross-country race where you have to work out your own course from the map and compass and it is now so popular that there is talk of including it in the Olympic Games.

Tough moorland

There is a good deal of pretty tough moorland in Britain. This is country which is not as spectacular as the mountains of the Lakes or Snowdonia. It often consists of miles of rolling moorland, all heather and tussock grass, with plenty of bog and sometimes weird rock outcrops known as tors or edges. On some of the moors – Kinder in the Peak District, for example – the peaty surface has been eroded into deep channels known as groughs which can be 20 or 30 feet (6–9 m) wide and 15 feet (4·5 m) deep, making the moor resemble a shell-scarred battlefield.

Walking in such country can be very hard going: heather clings to your trouser legs, tussock grass twists your ankles and it is easy to

Tough walking on the wild Pennine moors.

go over the boot tops in bog. Added to this is the usual absence of landmarks — just desolate moor to the horizon — which means you need to be able to use your map and compass.

Yet walking in such places is very popular because of the challenge if offers. There are some traditional walks in the Pennines, for example, which are long and arduous like the Marsden—Edale which crosses three tough moors — Black Hill, Bleaklow and Kinder Scout. A nickname for walkers who tackle routes like this is 'Bogtrotters'.

On the heights

3

Careful planning for walks

Mountain features

Mountain rescue

Bigger hills

The biggest mountains in Britain are those in Scotland, Snowdonia, and the Lake District. Though steep, many of them can be climbed just by walking up, so provided you have the right gear and know how to use a map and compass there is nothing to prevent you making an ascent. But not all of them are easy: Tryfan, in Snowdonia, practically demands the use of hands as well as feet no matter which way you try to climb it, and some of the Scottish mountains are very tough indeed.

Even where it might be easy to climb a mountain it can be difficult to link it to the next peak because the ridges in between might be tough going. Once you have climbed Tryfan, for example, if you wish to continue to the next peaks, the Glyders, you have to climb the rugged Bristly Ridge. In Scotland, some of the ridges are very difficult – those on Arran and Skye, for instance. You need a lot of experience before you can tackle these safely.

Of course, these difficult ways up are more interesting and exciting than the 'tourist routes'.

Route cards

Whenever you are planning a day out in the mountains it is useful to prepare a route card. This says where you are going and lists the 'legs' of the journey with compass bearing for each 'leg' and the time you estimate it will take to accomplish. A copy of this should be left at your starting place so that if there is a mishap and the rescue team have to look for you, they will know in which direction to concentrate their search. (Even if you do not make a route card you should always let someone know where you are going or, if you are camping, leave a note in the tent.)

Calculating the time taken for a journey is fairly simple if you use Naismith's Rule. A Scottish climber called Naismith worked out that on average one could climb at the rate of 3 miles per hour (4·8 kilometres per hour) plus an additional hour for every 2,000 ft (610 m) of ascent. (Reckon $\frac{1}{2}$ hr for descent.) Here is an example from the Lake District; a walk from Elterwater in Langdale to the Woolpack Inn in Eskdale —

Distance = 9 miles (14·4 km).
Height at Elterwater = 300 ft (91·4 km).
Highest point (Three Tarns) = 2,300 ft (701 m).
Height at Eskdale = 300 ft (91·4 m).
So, 9 mls (14·4 km) at 3 mph (4·8 kph) = 3 hrs
2,000 ft (701 m) ascent = 1 hr
2,000 ft (701 m) descent = $\frac{1}{2}$ hr
Total time needed = $3 + 1 + \frac{1}{2} = 4\frac{1}{2}$ hrs

Time must be added on for halts, and in bad weather it is useful to reckon on halving the climbing rate. If you try out Naismith's Rule on your local hills (but make the walk at least 7 miles or 11·2 kilometres) you can see how it suits your personal performance.

Mountain features

Once you get into the mountains you will quickly notice that there are many features which are fairly common. The accompanying photograph explains what these are called.

Ridges

Climbing a mountain such as Snowdon in Wales, or Ben Nevis in Scotland can be a very satisfying experience, but you will soon discover that linking several peaks together by their ridges is more fun. In the case of Snowdon, for example, you can start at the Youth Hostel at Pen y Pass and climb Crib Goch (3,023 ft or 921 m), then follow the ridge to Crib y ddysgl (3,493 ft or 1,065 m), then curve round to Snowdon summit (3,561 ft or 1,085 m) and finally to Y Lliwedd (2,947 ft or 898 m) before

*Mountain features.
Bowfell in the Lake
District. A path can be
seen leading up to the
ridge which rises to the
summit. Below the
ridge can be seen large
crags split by deep
gulleys. Scree lies
beneath the crags.*

*Crib Goch, an airy
ridge needing
determination on the
part of the walker.*

descending to Llyn Llydaw and Pen y Pass again. This walk is known as the Snowdon Horseshoe and once you have gained the top of Crib Goch you hardly ever descend below 3,000 ft (914 m) by more than a few feet. The effort involved in climbing the four peaks mentioned is much less than it would be if you attempted to climb each one separately.

This is known as ridge walking, and it is the usual sort of walk undertaken by experienced mountain walkers.

Sometimes the ridges are very easy and broad, but sometimes they are narrow and 'airy' — the ridge from Crib Goch to Crib y ddysgl comes into this latter class. Such a ridge has to be taken very steadily, and in bad weather, or when the ridge is iced, should be avoided.

Gulleys

These deep fissures in the mountainside sometimes provide an interesting way up (or down) but they always need treating with care. Some gulleys are real rock climbs, very steep and difficult — never try to climb or descend an unknown gulley unless you can see the whole length of it and there is an obvious way through.

Gulleys are often filled with scree and even when they are not may well have loose stones in them. This means that you must be careful not to dislodge any of these stones because if they go bouncing down the gulley they may strike someone else lower down. Remember that in a gulley you are trapped — there isn't much room for dodging missiles! If a party of walkers are ascending or descending a gulley, they should all keep close together. Can you see why?

Scree

Though mountain crags seem so strong and permanent they are in fact being worn away by the action of the weather. Bits break off from time to time and roll to the bottom of the crag. Over a course of centuries these bits pile up into long slopes of loose stones known as scree.

Scree can vary enormously in size from big blocks to tiny pieces no larger than a pea. At some time or another a mountaineer has to cross scree and the way he does it depends on the size of the pieces. If it is large blocks he can hop from one to another, landing lightly and skipping on to the next. A certain skill is required in this, and judgment too, because the blocks may not be stable. Similarly, when climbing up scree, a party should stay close together in case a loose block tumbles down.

Climbing small scree is very tiring — it always seems like one step up and two back — but small scree can be useful in descent because it offers a quick way down. A series of short jumps down the scree is known as scree-running and carries you to the bottom of the scree slope in no time. But note — it is *not* running in the proper sense (perhaps it should be called scree-jumping?) because you will remember what we learnt earlier about running down hills and how dangerous it could be.

Mist
If you have learned to use a map and compass properly a moorland mist should be no problem providing you take reasonable care — you should be able to navigate your way out of trouble. But in the

Mist can be dangerous.

big mountains it may not be so simple. You may be in an area which is extremely rocky, where to move in the wrong direction, even by a few feet, could be dangerous.

You have to make a decision which is based on the circumstances at the time. There is no easy answer to the problem of mist. What you must consider is whether the mist is likely to move soon (it could be just a cloud drifting over) and if so, whether you can sit it out. This is the safest, but you have to decide how long you can wait — for example, how long it will be to nightfall.

If you must move then aim carefully for the least craggy side of the mountain and descend that — even if it leads to the wrong valley. This may mean a long walk back to camp or hostel, but it is the only safe way.

A party should keep together in single file so that each person can see the one in front of him. With a Silva compass the leader should have no navigational problems, but a useful check can be made by the man at the back if he also carries one.

Benightment

In mountain ranges such as the Alps where routes can be long and hard, climbers frequently bivouac. This means they sleep out under the stars on some ledge, keeping warm by means of eiderdown clothing known as *duvets* (from the French for eiderdown). They take with them lightweight cooking gear.

Bivouacking is rarely necessary in Britain, though some people do it for fun. Much more common is the involuntary bivouac, or benightment, caused by over-ambitious planning, bad route finding, bad weather, or some minor accident which has slowed down the party.

In summer it would be foolish to go out on our hills equipped with all the gear necessary for a bivouac! So what do you do if you find yourself benighted?

If it is easy ground, with a path, then it is not too difficult to keep going with the aid of a torch, or even moonlight on some nights. Some walkers even practise night walks to test their navigation! But if the ground is dangerous you must bivouac.

The essential thing is to conserve body heat and prevent exposure. If a wind is blowing shelter must be found behind a wall or boulder, or it may be possible to make a rough sheltering wall from stones lying about. A couch of heather or bracken insulates the body from the ground. Every scrap of clothing should be worn and members of a party should huddle together for mutual warmth.

First aid

No matter how careful you are in the mountains minor accidents will happen — cuts and grazes, sprains and so on. Everyone who walks or climbs should carry a small personal first aid kit to deal with such emergencies. Where there is a group of three or more, a more ambitious first aid kit can be carried on a shared basis *in addition to the personal kits.*

The following items make up a simple first aid kit: triangular bandage, sterile dressing (wound dressing), lint, a broad and a narrow bandage, elastoplast in various sizes, antiseptic cream, safety pins. Aspirin can be useful, too, but should be used sparingly. Though not strictly first aid kit, we can include a penknife, matches, and a small torch.

I wonder if you can work out what each of the above items might be used for? What additional items do you feel ought to go into the group first aid kit?

A knowledge of first aid is invaluable and well worth learning.

Mountain rescue

In all the mountainous areas of Britain there are mountain rescue teams ready at short notice to go to the aid of injured climbers or walkers. The 'injury' might not be a broken leg or anything so dramatic: it might be exposure or simply a bad sprain — anything, in fact, which prevents the person from moving. The teams also go to the rescue of climbers who are stuck on a cliff and they search for missing walkers. All the members of a team are local volunteers with a lot of mountaineering experience. They practise rescue techniques in the mountains, just as lifeboatmen practise rescues at sea, so that they know exactly what to do in any emergency.

They are equipped with Land Rovers, radios and special stretchers adapted for mountain country — though the days of the long carry are mostly gone because it is more usual to radio for a helicopter nowadays. The teams work in co-operation with the police and, if necessary, the RAF Mountain Rescue service. In addition, some dogs have been trained to search and find victims buried in snow avalanches.

The equipment is kept at Mountain Rescue Posts (often an inn or Youth Hostel) and all such posts are marked with a special badge of a blue circle and red cross bearing the words MOUNTAIN RESCUE POST. They are indicated on Ordnance Survey maps.

A mountain rescue team in action.

What to do in case of accident

Helicopters are often used in mountain rescue. This one is in the French Alps.

If help is needed from the valley several things have to be considered. First the victim must be made comfortable and kept warm. It is necessary to guard against exposure because it might be hours before the rescue team arrives. If the accident has involved a fall it is better not to try and move the victim if you suspect spinal injury. On the other hand, he may have fallen into a spot which is itself dangerous, such as a narrow ledge. If a rope is available he should be made secure against further fall. Often it is a matter of weighing one consideration against another and doing what seems best.

In a large party it is the leader's job to see that all the other members of the group are conducted to safety.

In a group someone should stay with the victim to comfort him whilst the two strongest members descend to the valley to fetch help. If only one person is available to descend to the valley his first consideration must be for his own safety — he must reach the valley, even though his caution costs extra time. Where there are only two in the party then the injured one must be made warm and comfortable as mentioned above, and his position marked by something obvious, which the rescue team can spot easily — a red anorak, for instance. His companion must then make a cautious descent.

On reaching the valley make immediate contact with the authorities either by going to a rescue post, if one is near, or contacting the police by phone. It is essential to tell the rescuers exactly where the victim lies and how to identify the place. A team leader who has sent a runner down to the valley will normally write a description of the accident place, including map references, for the runner to carry down.

The distress signal

One of the problems of a small party is that in the event of an accident, getting help is more difficult and dangerous, as you will have realised from what has already been said above. But help might be quite near at hand — there might be others on the same mountain quite unaware of the difficulties you are in. So an international signal has been devised: six long blasts on a whistle, followed by a minute's pause then repeated (or at night, six long flashes from a torch in the same manner). If it is heard help will be forthcoming at once — all mountaineers respond to this signal immediately because it is an unwritten rule of mountaineering that you should stop what you are doing and go to the help of others. After all, it might be you next time! Obviously, whistles should never be blown for 'fun' in the hills — you are likely to be surrounded by groups of angry mountaineers in no time.

Rock for climbing

4

Rock for climbing

Using the rope

Special techniques

There are any number of ridges in our British hills which are so narrow that you are forced to use your hands as well as feet. In the previous chapter Crib Goch on the Snowdon Horseshoe was mentioned; then there is the North Ridge of Tryfan, the Bristly Ridge and several others in Wales. In the Lakes there is Sharp Edge on Blencathra or Striding Edge on Helvellyn, whilst in Scotland there are so many ridges of this kind it would need a whole chapter just to list them all!

When you have to use your hands, either to steady yourself or pull yourself up, it is called scrambling and it is a sort of half-way stage between walking and rock-climbing. Not all scrambling is on ridges — in the Lake District, for example, there is a famous scramble called Jack's Rake which leads up a huge cliff.

Scrambling needs a steady head. If you come across a scramble you can't do straight off keep trying — each time you will get a little further. Don't grab at the rock — look round for holds, test them to make sure they are sound and step up a short distance. Then pause and work out the next step and so on. If you keep calm you will get over the obstacle.

Gear for rock climbing

For rock climbing you need all the gear mentioned for walking (because many of the crags are in out-of-the-way places and you need to be a walker to reach them) and also the special gear which a climber uses for protection against a fall.

The sort of boots used for walking, with Vibram soles, are good enough for simple climbs. Climbers call these 'bendy boots' — can you think why? Gym shoes and training shoes can also be used for easy climbs, but the best footwear is a canvas-topped boot known as a P.A. after Pierre Allain, the French climber who invented them. P.A.'s have a smooth rubber sole stiffened inside by a steel or plastic shank to make them rigid. They lace right down to the toes and are generally tight fitting — they are very uncomfortable to walk in for any distance. The advantage of the P.A. is that it gives superb friction and a positive grip on very small holds.

Perhaps the single most important item of gear for a rock climber is his rope. How he uses this we will see later, but it has to be a nylon rope because only nylon has the strength required. Usually it is 11 mm diameter and 40 or 50 metres long.

The climber may tie on to the rope directly but nowadays it is more usual to use a harness made of webbing because this protects him from the shock of the rope if he should fall off. He is also likely to have some loops of nylon tape, called slings, some special steel or alloy links called karabiners, and some metal pieces known as chocks, possibly threaded with wire. If the climb is a particularly serious one he may also carry some metal spikes for driving into cracks — these are called pitons, or pegs, and he will need a piton hammer to drive them in.

Because most injuries to climbers are head injuries it is sensible to wear a climbing helmet. This not only protects the head in the event of a fall but also protects it against stones falling from above.

All this equipment is shown in the accompanying pictures.

What is a rock climb?
The difference between scrambling and the easiest rock climbs is very little — scrambling often borders on climbing and, as a matter of fact, in the early days of the sport climbing was often called scrambling. A modern rock climb is something very different, however. A climb is a route up a steep rock feature where all four limbs are constantly in action (though there will probably be resting places). It demands good balance and nerve in a struggle against gravity.

If it is a short climb of, say, 50 ft (15·2 m), such as may be found on many small outcrops of rock, it will usually be climbed in one go, from bottom to top. This is called a single pitch. On the bigger climbs there are many pitches, one after another, with resting places called stances in between.

A climb becomes more difficult if the holds are small and widely spaced, or awkwardly placed. Perhaps the rock is not too sound, or the pitches are long and unprotected (see p. 48).

In this country climbers grade the climbs according to difficulty: Moderate, Difficult, Very Difficult, Severe, Very Severe, Extremely Severe. Sometimes the word Hard is added if the climb is tough for its grade – for example, Hard Severe means the climb is harder than usual for a Severe, but not quite hard enough for a Very Severe.

All climbs have a name too. This might be something rather dull like North Rib or Route One but often it might be descriptive or humorous. A famous climb on Gimmer Crag in the Lake District is called Kipling's Groove – because it was 'ruddy hard'. Get it?

In climbers' guidebooks you will find names, grades and a description of the routes. Sometimes the guidebook also tells you who first did the climb (called a first ascent) and when.

Climbing is a challenge and the better you become at it the harder the climbs you can manage. All climbers like to be the first to do a climb, make a first ascent – particularly if it is one which has been tried by other climbers!

Using the rope
The rope is the climber's lifeline. It stops his fall if he comes off, or at least, reduces the distance he will go. He does not climb up the rope, as some people think, but takes it up with him as he climbs the rock. After all, he is a rock climber, not a rope climber.

A rock-climbing team is known as a 'rope' (confusing!) and consists of two or three persons. The man who is going to climb first is called the leader, and the other is called the second. If there are three then the third man is called 'last man'.

The leader is belayed to the wall behind and brings up the second man. A very severe quarry climb.

The leader ties on to the rope and climbs the first pitch. At the top of this he will find a ledge, perhaps only a small one, where he can stand. With the aid of a sling he attaches himself to a spike of rock in such a way that he cannot be pulled off his stance no matter what happens. He then takes in the spare rope and calls for the second to follow. As the second climbs the leader continues to take in the rope. Eventually the second man joins the leader, and he too ties on to the rock. Both men are now secure on the ledge — this is called belaying.

They then repeat this for the next pitch, and so on to the end of the climb. If there is a third man he too joins them on the ledge at the top of the first pitch, brought up by the second. If it is a small ledge the leader might decide to go on up the next pitch before the last man comes up, but whatever is decided only one man climbs at a time — the other two are securely belayed.

Taking in and paying out

Once the leader has reached his stance he takes in any spare rope left between himself and the second man below. It may be he cannot actually see him so when all the rope is pulled in the second calls out 'That's me!' The leader shouts back 'Climb when you're ready!' and as the second starts on the rock he replies 'Climbing!' In this way each knows just what the other is doing.

The second climbs the rock and the leader takes in the rope between them as he does so. He does not pull the second up, neither does he allow the rope to be so slack that it gets in the climber's way. You can see that because the rope is protecting him from falling, the second is reasonably safe, but in fact if the leader just held the rope in his hands the energy of the falling climber might rip it through his hands and he would have to let go. To prevent this happening he passes the rope round his back at waist level, so that the friction of the rope against his clothing acts as an extra brake. Recently, special gadgets have been invented to help him hold the rope, but many climbers still use the traditional method.

Similarly, when the leader climbs the second pays out the rope round his waist so that he has the extra friction in the event of a fall.

Top roping

Obviously, the safest way to practise climbing is always to be a
second because then you are always protected by the rope above.
On many small outcrops it is possible for someone to walk up to
the top, belay in the usual way, then drop the spare end of the rope
down the crag so that his companions can tie on in turn and do the
climb. This is known as 'top roping' and is often used by
instructors when they are training beginners because it is quick
and more climbing gets done. On bigger crags top roping is not
possible, and I am sure you can see why.

*A typical Sunday at
Harrison's Rocks in
Kent, popular practice
rocks. Top roping is
extensively used here.*

Birch Tree Wall, Black Rocks, Derbyshire. The climber traverses along a sloping ledge. Notice his runners.

Protecting the leader

Once past the beginner's stage, however, most climbers like to be leader on a climb because the leader accepts the greatest challenge and has the biggest thrill. It will no doubt have occurred to you that the risk accepted by the leader is greater than that of the second. The leader has no rope above him for protection – in fact, he is the one taking the rope up – so how can it help him?

Well, he tries to arrange for his own protection by a series of 'running belays'. Some of these are shown in the pictures and you will see at once how they work, but here's an example. Suppose the leader has climbed some 25 feet (7–8 m) up the rocks. If he falls off he is going to hit the ground very hard and possibly injure himself severely. But at that moment he spies a spike of rock near at hand round which he can slip a tape sling. This he does and he joins the sling to his rope by means of a karabiner. Now if he falls the sling will stop him going too far. A few feet further on he will place another running belay, and so on, so that he never has far to fall.

But what if there are no spikes? Well, there may be a crack into which he can place one of his metal chocks. This chock will be attached to a sling (or wire) and again he clips his rope to it by means of a karabiner. If he falls, the chock will jam in the crack and hold him.

On some specially hard climbs where there are no cracks big enough for chocks and no spikes, the climber might bang in a piton and clip on to that for protection, but only in extreme cases. Pitons damage the rock, eventually spoiling the route for other climbers (and leaving nasty unsightly scars on the crag) so they are only used when absolutely necessary.

Strangely enough there are climbs, even some reasonably easy ones, with pitches which just do not lend themselves to any of these tactics. Such a pitch is said to be 'unprotected' – and the leader must make quite sure he doesn't fall off!

Holds

The difficulty of a climb depends upon the kind of holds it provides for hands and feet. An easy climb may be fairly steep but you can guarantee that there will be plenty of holds, probably fairly big ones and incut. Incut holds are the sort you can curl your fingers over to get a good grip. If they are very big and very good, climbers call them 'jug handles' or 'jugs'.

On harder climbs the holds will be smaller — perhaps just allowing the tips of your fingers to grip them. In some cases they may even slope the wrong way so that a climber using them has to rely on pressure alone. Nor are all holds horizontal — sometimes they slope awkwardly or they are vertical and have to be used for a sideways pull or push. Thinking out how to use these various holds is part of the skill of climbing.

What else about holds does a climber need to consider? Well, he will need to figure out the combination, that is to say, in which order he intends using them. If he starts off on the wrong foot, for example, he might find the whole problem much harder than it need be. He must also make sure that the holds are sound and not likely to come away in his hands.

Balance
Good balance is the key to stylish climbing. At its simplest level it means keeping your body away from the rock, using hand holds which are about shoulder height and stepping up gradually and calmly. If the rock lies back at a fairly easy angle (a slab, climbers call it) your hands may be used simply to hold yourself in balance, without any need to pull up. It is much less strenuous to let your legs do the work, because they are stronger than your arms. Climbs which involve a lot of arm work are said to be 'strenuous'.

Once you are established on the rock you have four points of contact keeping you in balance — two hands and two feet. Wherever possible a move should only require you to change one of these at a time — that is, you keep three points firmly on the rock.

Mantelshelf
A special move called a mantelshelf has to be made from time to time. There may be a flat hold about chest height with the next hold above it well out of reach. The trick is to do a press up onto the

Balance on a slab.

flat hold until you can get your feet onto it and then straighten up.
It requires delicate balance.

Cracks

Sometimes the only way to climb a pitch is by means of a crack in it
because the rock itself is holdless. If the crack is wide it is called a
chimney (remember how in the old days little boys were used as
chimney sweeps?). A wide chimney can be bridged, that is, a foot

put on either side of it. If it is not quite so wide, or has fewer holds it can be climbed 'back and knee' in which case your back goes against one wall and your knees against the other and you shuffle up. You can actually rest in the back and knee position if you wish, which is just as well because it is a tiring method of climbing! Some narrow chimneys are climbed by just wriggling up — thrutching, climbers call it.

Where a crack is too narrow to allow your body inside it then there are three possible ways it might be climbed. The easiest (and

Bridging a chimney.

Backing up a wide chimney.

commonest) is simply to use the edges of the crack as ordinary holds and climb it accordingly. If this is not possible then jamming might be the answer. Foot jamming is self-explanatory — you just jam your foot in the crack until it sticks there (taking care you can get it out again!). Hand jamming is more difficult. Here you must slot your hand into the crack then push your thumb across the palm jamming the hand in the crack. You then pull up on the jammed hand. The third method can be used with a corner crack and is known as a layback. In this you put your feet on the opposite wall and pull at the crack, then move up feet and hands alternately. It is an extremely tiring method of climbing.

Another tiring exercise, sometimes necessary on horizontal cracks, is a hand traverse. This means you just swing across the rocks sideways on hands alone, a bit like Tarzan. Before embarking on a hard traverse it is doubly necessary to work every move out in advance — there is not often a second chance!

A young leader in action. Note the runner for protection.

Artificial climbing

If the rock is completely without holds, or if it juts out in an overhang, then ordinary climbing methods are not sufficient. To overcome such problems 'artificial climbing' methods are used. Pitons are driven into thin cracks and little rope ladders consisting of three or four alloy steps are hung from them, so that the climber can climb the ladder, gaining a few feet until he can hang another little ladder from the next piton. He climbs up again and takes the first little ladder with him — and so it goes on until either the climb finishes or the rock relents and he is able to climb 'free' again. The little ladders are known as etriers, and sometimes they are just knotted loops of tape.

Where the rock is completely blank the only way up is to drill small holes in the rock and plug in special expansion bolts from which to hang the etriers.

As you may easily imagine, artificial climbing can be a long, tiring business, especially if any bolting has to be done. Handling the ropes can be tricky too. Few climbers in Britain bother with it.

Abseiling

Pronounced 'ab-sile-ing', this is from a German word which means descending by rope; in other words, sliding down. Only the sliding is done in a controlled fashion so that the climber doesn't burn his hands by rope friction, or fall off. It is a very quick way down a crag. Some sea cliffs can only be reached by abseils from the cliff top.

Nowadays there are many ways of abseiling, but they all depend upon the friction of the rope around the body or around the abseiling device to control descent.

The simplest method requires nothing but the rope itself. What you do is double the rope, putting the loop round a stout tree or rock spike and throwing the free ends down the crag. Standing astride the rope you then pick it up from behind and loop it across your chest and over your shoulder (see picture). You then simply walk backwards down the cliff!

Amazingly, it really does work, though the first time you try it you

A classic abseil down on of the many artificial climbing walls now available.

will be scared stiff! A number of precautions are needed — for example, the rope must reach the ground below or a ledge, and it must not ride off its anchor point. Anyone learning abseiling should have the additional protection of a top rope — it is very easy to make a careless mistake, and abseiling accidents are quite common.

This method is called the 'classic abseil' and though simple is not very comfortable. Nowadays climbers usually use a device called a 'descendeur'.

Warning!
Rock climbing is great fun and an exciting sport but it is also dangerous. The penalties for mistakes are often severe. This is why it must be learnt properly, with qualified, experienced instructors.

Winter

5

Winter in the mountains

Using an ice axe

Avalanches

When the hills are gripped in the frosts of winter they change character completely. A fall of snow transforms them into a magic fairyland landscape, very beautiful — and very dangerous.

The dangers are three-fold. First, and most common, because air temperatures are colder during winter months, the effect of a breeze is much more severe; in other words, there is a greater

Winter in the mountains. Lochnagar in Scotland.

chance of exposure. There may also be a chance of frostbite. Second, the hours of daylight are shorter in winter and a carelessly planned expedition can more easily lead to benightment — and a winter bivouac is a very much more arduous experience than a summer bivouac. Third, the ground itself can be more difficult to cross — icy patches make steep hillsides dangerous; ice can glaze the rocks on ridges or even scree, turning a summer scramble into a desperate undertaking; snow can obscure obstacles, make

A duvet jacket.

movement difficult and even, sometimes, avalanche. A winter mountaineer needs to take all these things into consideration before he sets out into the hills.

Winter wear

In chapter 2 you read about the sort of clothing necessary for summer hill walking and climbing. In winter you need the same gear but with some additions to combat the extra cold. For example, a balaclava helmet and gloves which *may* be useful in summer become essential in winter. Both should be made of wool – remember, wool for warmth. Similarly, an extra wool sweater is useful and in this case two light wool sweaters are better than one heavy thick one – can you think why?

The problem with wool gloves, if there is snow around, is that they soon become wet and uncomfortable, and if there is a wind blowing the chilling effect on finger tips is quite painful. This can be largely overcome by a pair of waterproof and windproof overmitts which are worn over the gloves. In fact, climbers who are undertaking steep snow and ice climbs where they are handling snow for hours on end often wear three pairs – a pair of light wool gloves, a pair of oiled wool mitts over the gloves, and a pair of overmitts over all.

But what about the lower limbs? Well, it is possible to protect your legs from cold in just the same way as your hands, that is, by adding extra layers. In this case you wear long thermal underwear beneath your breeches (or a pair of pyjama bottoms makes a good substitute) and windproof overtrousers on top.

Duvet

For climbs in the Himalayas or winter climbs in the Alps, where the mountains are much higher than they are in Britain and the cold more intense, specially warm clothing has been developed. It is known as *duvet* gear (from the French word meaning eiderdown), and as the name suggests, it is made from down-filled material. Perhaps you have come across *duvets* at home? The same material is used in making Continental Quilts which are very popular for beds.

Duvet can be made into jackets with hoods, trousers, gloves and even little bags in which you can put your feet if you have to bivouac. These latter are called *pied d'éléphant* — elephant's foot! Dressed in *duvet* jacket and trousers you look a bit like the man in the Michelin tyre advert. Nevertheless, they are very warm.

Many climbers wear *duvet* jackets in this country during the winter. Cagoules are made on the generous side so they will fit over *duvet* jackets.

Frostbite

In intensely cold weather extremities of the body such as ears, nose, fingers and toes can suffer from frostbite. The tiny capillaries close, cutting off the blood which supplies oxygen, and ice crystals form between the cells. The affected part turns putty-coloured and goes numb.

Real frostbite is fairly rare in Britain because if sensible precautions are taken it should always be avoidable, but minor frostbite, especially to fingers, is common enough. The immediate treatment is to warm them — pushing your hands down your breeches is a good way.

It is really quite painful as the blood comes back — like severe pins and needles.

Benightment

Benightment in winter can be a very serious affair. It can be made more bearable by carrying plenty of extra clothing (*duvet* is ideal, of course) and by also carrying a down sleeping bag. A primus stove and pan, for making hot drinks, is a further help. Obviously a tent would be better still — but here we come up against a problem, which is this: the more weight you have to carry, the slower you will travel and the slower you travel, the more chance there is of being overtaken by darkness. The real answer is to work out your route in detail, start early and don't dawdle.

A good party leader will also bear in mind 'escape routes', that is, ways to cut short the walk if he finds that the party is taking longer than he estimated.

Snow holes

A snow hole.

If there is deep snow on the mountains one way of making benightment safer is to dig a snow hole. To do this you choose a steep bank where the snow lies deepest and dig two tunnels about 6 ft (2 m) apart, parallel with each other. After some 5 ft (1·5 m) of tunnelling the ends are joined by a cross-cut tunnel, so that you have a sort of snow cave with two entrances. You crawl into the cave and block the entrances with snow, or rucksacks, and make an air vent by pushing an ice axe through the roof to make a small hole.

Such a snow hole can become quite warm (if damp!) and will certainly keep the wind out. The trouble is, of course, that usually the only available tool for digging is an ice axe, and the job can take hours.

The ice axe
This very useful climbing tool is essential for safety whenever the hills are under snow. It consists of a shaft of ash or some strong synthetic laminate, about 65 cm (about 2·5 ft) long, at one end of which is a spike and ferrule and at the other end the axe head. You will see from the picture that it is really more like an adze than an axe. One end of the head is called the blade, and the other is called the pick. The axe usually has a wrist strap attached so that if it is dropped accidentally it won't be lost.

For hill walkers the chief value of the ice axe is that it can be used as a brake in the event of a fall. If you come off and find yourself sliding down steep snow, you roll over onto the axe which is held across the chest and press the pick into the snow. This must be done gradually or the axe will be snatched from your grasp.

Anyone venturing into the hills in winter should practise this 'self arrest' technique on an easy snow slope.

Climbing easy snow slopes
Going up a snow slope you can kick your boot toes into the snow, making a step. You hold the ice axe across your chest in a position ready for braking, should you slip. Going across a slope you can use the side of your boot to kick a suitable little platform in the snow. If the snow is soft you will find that step kicking is no more than rather steady walking, but if the snow is more consolidated you may have to kick quite hard.

It is less tiring for other members of a party if they follow exactly in the steps made by their leader. If the going is hard, the lead can be changed from time to time so that everyone does his share of the work.

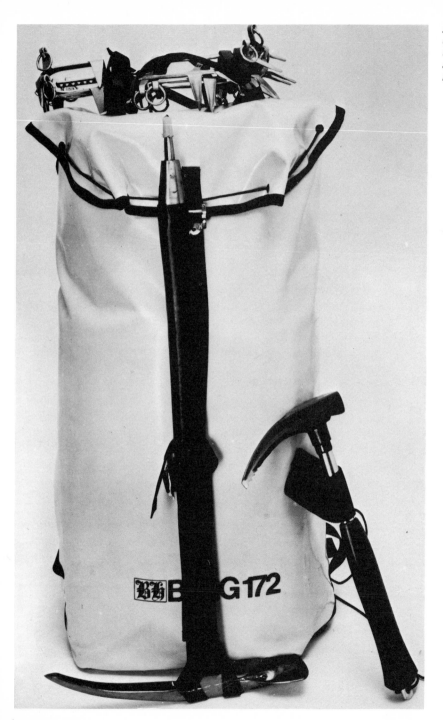

A rucksack equipped to carry crampons, an ice axe and ice hammer.

Descending easy snow slopes

The easiest way down is usually to follow the steps made on the way up, but it may well be that you intend to traverse the hill completely, descending by a different route. This time, of course, the steps are kicked using the heels of your boots.

If the snow is hard enough a very quick method of descent is to glissade. This means sliding down, using your boot soles like skis. It is done in a crouching position with the spike of the axe trailing behind in the snow, like the brake on a toboggan.

Glissading is good fun but it should only be attempted on clear slopes where you can see the full length of the glissade and after you have learnt how to brake a fall.

Snow conditions

Snow can change from day to day and even hour to hour according to the weather. What is a simple snow slope in the morning may turn into a sheet of ice by late afternoon. Constant wariness is essential.

Avalanches

When we think of avalanches we often think of high mountain ranges such as the Alps or Himalayas where huge avalanches are quite common. Some are big enough to flatten whole forests or devastate villages. The main damage is done by the mass of air which the avalanche pushes in front of it.

There are many smaller avalanches, though, and quite a few in Britain each winter. These may not create wide devastation but they are very dangerous for anyone trapped in them. The reasons why some snow slides away whilst some does not are too complicated to go into here and unfortunately there is no sure-fire way of telling an avalanche slope when you see one. What is certain is that an avalanche can happen even on a quite gentle slope — as little as 30°.

It is a good idea to keep away from snow slopes after a period of heavy rain, when the snow becomes slushy, and to give any fresh falls of snow at least two days to consolidate.

Steeper snow

Many gullies, especially in Scotland, give fine steep snow climbs.
Experienced climbers climb these 'alpine fashion', that is roped
together with 15 or 20 feet (4·5–6 m) of rope between them but
everyone moving together. If one man slips he is likely to pull the
others off and so they are always prepared to plunge their axe
shafts into the snow and whip the rope round them quickly. The
man who slips is, of course, braking hard with his axe.

*Steep snow climbing
in the Cairngorms.*

To climb together like this the members of a rope need great confidence in each other's ability. Surer, but slower, is to climb the gully in stages, like a rock climb. The leader goes up, plants his axe firmly in the snow and belays to it in the usual way. He takes in the rope as his second climbs. The second then plants his axe firmly, belays to it, and pays out the rope in the usual way as the leader does the next stretch. And so on to the top.

Unfortunately an ice axe stuck into the snow is not too safe as a belay and to overcome this problem a special snow anchor, known as a 'dead-man' (because it gets buried) has been developed. The dead-man consists of an alloy plate with a strong wire attached to the centre. The plate is buried at 40° in the snow and the climber belayed to the wire. If it is correctly placed it will hold a very large sudden shock — but practice in placing them correctly is essential.

Crampons

Steep snow can be climbed in the same manner as described previously, that is, by kicking steps. If it becomes too hard, however, the steps may have to be chopped out of the snow with the blade of the ice axe. This is very time-consuming, and remember, time is very vital during short winter days.

To overcome this climbers wear spikes on their boots. The spikes are called crampons and they enable the climber to move over hard snow (or even ice) without kicking or cutting steps at all. He just relies on the spikes sticking into the hard snow to hold him.

It is really quite remarkable the confidence which a pair of crampons gives in icy conditions. Remember — they give speed as well as security, which is why many hill walkers have taken to using them, even though they may not be climbing anything steep.

Ice climbing

Not all gullies are steep snow slopes. Sometimes the snow is interrupted by a wall of ice, very steep and anything from 10 to 50 or more feet (3 to 15 m) high. Until recently, ice pitches like this had to be climbed by cutting hand and foot holds in the ice with

the pick of the ice axe — like cutting out a ladder in the ice. It was   *Climbing steep ice.*
time-consuming and nerve-racking. Nowadays climbers em-
barking on steep ice use a special method known as front-
pointing. They have two very short ice axes with special picks
which stick in the ice and they have two forward pointing spikes
on each crampon. They climb the ice by sticking axes and front-
points into the ice in turn.

Obviously, if a leader falls from an ice pitch he will not be able to
brake because the ice will be too hard and steep. He needs
protection just like a rock-climbing leader. To get this he uses ice
screws, which are pitons he can literally screw into the ice. He
clips a karabiner onto the ice screw and passes his rope through it,
so making a running belay for himself.

In ice climbing, like rock climbing, only one man moves at a time.
The others are belayed, either to natural belays, pitons, ice screws
or dead-men.

6   How to find out more

Organisations

British Mountaineering Council (BMC), Crawford House, Precinct Centre, Booth Street East, Manchester 13.

Camping Club of Great Britain and Ireland Ltd, 11 Lower Grosvenor Place, London SW1.

Mountain Leadership Training Board, Crawford House, Precinct Centre, Booth Street East, Manchester 13.

Outward Bound Trust, 73 Great Peter Street, London SW1.

Ramblers' Association, 1 Crawford Mews, London W1.

Youth Hostels Association
   (1) England and Wales — YHA, Trevelyan House, St Albans, Herts.
   (2) Scotland — SYHA, 7 Bruntsfield Crescent, Edinburgh 10.
   (3) Ulster — YHA NI, 28 Bedford Street, Belfast.
   (4) Ireland — An Oige, 39 Mountjoy Square, Dublin 1.

National Mountaineering Centres

England and Wales — Plas y Brenin, National Mountaineering Centre, Capel Curig, North Wales.

Scotland — Glenmore Lodge, Aviemore, Inverness-shire.

(N.B. There are many more outdoor pursuits centres owned by local authorities.)

Films and filmstrips

The BMC (address above) will supply a list of available films and filmstrips on application (send s.a.e.).

Magazines

Climber and Rambler (monthly)

The official magazine of the BMC covers all aspects of mountaineering, mainly in Britain and Europe.

Mountain (bi-monthly)
A magazine with an international readership devoted to high standard climbing.

Pamphlets, etc.
Mountain Rescue Handbook – Mountain Rescue Committee.
Safety on Mountains – BMC
Junior First Aid – British Red Cross Society.
ABC of First Aid – British Red Cross Society.
Exposure – Climber and Rambler Magazine.

Guidebooks
Every mountain area in Britain has one or more guidebooks, and there are also special climbers' guidebooks for rock climbs. There are several hundred in all. The BMC will advise on which guidebooks cover any particular area.

Books
Of the thousands of titles dealing with mountains and climbers the following are only a brief, but useful, selection.

Technique
Mountaineering – A. Blackshaw (Penguin, 1970).
Mountain Leadership – E. Langmuir (BMC).
The Book of Rock Climbing – W. Unsworth (Barker, 1968).
Big Wall Climbing – D. Scott (Kaye & Ward, 1974).
Backpacking in Britain – D. Booth (Oxford Illustrated Press, 1974).
Backpacking – Peter Lumley (English Universities Press, 1974).

General
Encyclopaedia of Mountaineering – W. Unsworth (Hale, 1975) (Penguin).
World Atlas of Mountaineering – Noyce and McMorrin (Nelson, 1969).
Hard Rock – K. Wilson (Granada, 1974).

Because it is There — W. Unsworth (Gollancz, 1968).

The Mountaineer's Companion — M. Ward (Eyre & Spottis-woode, 1966).

Mountaineering in Scotland — W. H. Murray (Dent, 1962).

Mountaineering in Britain — Clark and Pyatt (Phoenix House, 1957).

Two Star Red — Gwen Moffat (Hodder & Stoughton, 1964).

I Chose to Climb — C. Bonington (Gollancz, 1966) (Penguin).

The Hard Years — J. Brown (Gollancz, 1967) (Penguin).